THE HOT DRINK
·BOOK·

THE HOT DRINK ·BOOK·

NONI SCOTT

Delicious alcohol-free recipes for every
taste and season

First published in Great Britain by
The Bath Street Press
1–5 Bath St, London EC1V 9LB

© 1988 (text) Noni Scott
© 1988 (illustrations) Chloë Cheese
© 1988 (this edition) The Bath Street Press

The Bath Street Press is a subsidiary of Marshall Pickering Holdings Ltd,
3 Beggarwood Lane, Basingstoke RG23 7LP

British Library Cataloguing in Publication Data

Scott, Oenone
The hot drink book.
1. Drinks – Recipes
I. Title
641.8′7

ISBN 1–85420–011–9

Designed by Peter Laws
Typesetting by TJB Photosetting Ltd., South Witham, Lincolnshire
Printed and bound in Italy by New Interlitho spa.

Contents

INTRODUCTION

We all know, and appreciate, the comfort and enjoyment provided by a cup of tea, coffee or hot chocolate. But the increasing availability of exotic fruits, herbs and spices is changing not only cooking but the drinking habits of a lifetime.

The traditional benefits of herbs have always been available for those with a little knowledge, and the tisane-drinking French have been extolling their virtues for centuries. Now we can all try unusual, exciting delicious drinks, which soothe minor ailments, pep us up and leave

HOT TIPS

Herbs

When herbs are dried the flavour is concentrated, so if you are using fresh herbs you will need slightly more than if they were dried. The flavour of drinks made with fresh herbs is quite different. Try them both and find out which you prefer.

Milk

With the exception of Rooibosch, avoid adding milk to herb teas. Milk changes the flavour and cools the drink. Instead, cool the tea by serving in wide shallow bowls.

Moderation

Whether you are keen on hot chocolate or herb teas remember the old saw 'in measure is treasure'. Vary your drinks to get the most benefit from them, particularly the herbal variety. Consult a medical herbalist if you need treatment for a particular disorder and be especially moderate in your drinking habits if you are pregnant.

Quantity

Do not be put off if you do not fall in love with your first taste of a new drink. You can always combine a herb you trust with an untried one, or several. For instance try camomile, mint and cinnamon. Be creative! You can also vary the quantities. It is always better to start with small quantities and weak mixtures. If you use too large a quantity the taste can be bitter and lack subtlety.

us tingling with a natural, healthy, alcohol-free glow. They are also a delightful change from an excess of 'instants'.

Why *hot* drinks? Certainly not because they are only suitable for cold northern countries. In India, Africa and the Far East the cuppa is traditionally served hot, and its function is to refresh and cool down. Many of the drinks in this book can be drunk cold, too, but they are so delicious you will want to taste them long before they cool!

Sugar	In several of the recipes I have used sugar, but remember that the health value of herb teas is reduced by adding sugar. Use honey instead or try fig or date syrup.
Tea	I have used the word tea to include tisanes and infusions made with herbs as well as true teas made from the leaves of the camellia bush family. Tea experts disapprove of the name tea being given to infusions which contain no tannin. They prefer these to be called tisanes.
Teapots	When you really start to enjoy herbal teas, buy a special infuser with a built-in strainer, or use a special teapot to avoid imparting a strange flavour to other teas.
Water	Some connoisseurs use their favourite still mineral water in preference to tap water, especially if they live in an area with lime or chalky water. Water which has been filtered is a good alternative. This also helps to avoid scum. For leaf and flower herb teas it is best to use water which has just boiled but is not still bubbling. So count to five after the water has boiled before pouring on to tea.

EARLY
MORNING

Before you start
planning or worrying about how you are going to
organize your day, slip out of bed and make one of
these reassuring drinks. Better still, persuade
someone else to bring you a cup. While some purists
regularly clear their systems by drinking hot water
with a slice of lemon, these suggestions cater for
more adventurous palates.

MINT TEA

Culpeper claims that mint 'stirs up bodily lust; therefore too much must not be taken, because it makes the blood thin'. It certainly leaves your breath sweet and is said to relieve most ailments from headaches and nausea to flatulence.

Each mint has a slightly different flavour. Water mint is the most common wild form, spearmint thrives everywhere and peppermint is found particularly in the South and West. If you have none, beg a root from a neighbour. It will grow happily in a window-box or plant pot.

INGREDIENTS FOR TWO

25g (1oz) of fresh or 2 teaspoons dried mint

450ml (¾ pint) boiling water

METHOD

Remove thick stalks of fresh mint, rinse leaves and place in warmed pot. Pour in boiled water. Infuse for five minutes under tea cosy. Strain into glass or cup. Garnish with lemon slice if preferred. Some people like to add sugar.

CAMOMILE TEA

Camomile is one of the most popular herbs and is easily grown. At Buckingham Palace there is a camomile lawn, and when you walk on camomile its fragrance perfumes the air. So, for a right royal beginning to the day, try this soothing tea which is reputed to relieve digestive disturbances, mild period pains and headaches and have sedative properties. It is also helpful to children suffering from colic. As an early morning drink, it also allays nausea.

If you add a sprinkling of ginger to camomile tea it makes you perspire and will help sweat away those nasty winter colds. Camomile makes a useful appetizer, so if you need to eat breakfast, but often cannot face it, camomile may help.

You need to pick a lot of flower heads for camomile tea, but they keep well in an airtight jar. The true camomile, *matricaria chamomilla*, is said to have the best flavour.

INGREDIENTS FOR TWO

2 teaspoons dried camomile flowers

600ml (1 pint) boiling water

METHOD

Pour the boiled water on to the flowers in the warmed pot. Cover and leave for five or six minutes to infuse. Strain into cups. A sprinkling of marigold petals on top makes it a feast for the eyes, too.

ROSEHIP TEA

My favourite is a mixture of rosehip and hibiscus which makes the lovely colour. Another delicious combination is rosehip and orange (available from Whittards of Chelsea, London). Rosehip tea is remarkable for its scent, colour and quantity of vitamin C. Large doses of vitamin C help reduce the symptoms of some infections and colds. As it now seems clear that carbon monoxide destroys vitamin C you may need extra if you live in a town or near a motorway.

Unless you have endless patience, it is not worth picking the hips and spending hours boiling and sieving to get rid of their spiky hairs. Instead, buy already prepared rosehips from your local health shop.

INGREDIENTS FOR TWO

2 heaped teaspoons dried rosehips and hibiscus

600ml (1 pint) boiling water

METHOD

Pour boiled water onto the hips and hibiscus in the warmed pot. Leave to infuse for five minutes before straining into cups. For entertainment I sometimes pour the water directly on to the hips in warmed bowls so that I can watch them swelling and colouring the liquid to my favourite depth of pink. A quick dab with a spoon sinks any fragments floating on the top.

BREAKFAST

C

ut out the
habitual cup of instant tea or coffee at breakfast time
and try something a bit more adventurous presented
in a different cup or bowl. This will make even
Monday morning feel like the beginning of a holiday.

HOT CHOCOLATE
WITH ORANGE
PEEL

At the Mexican court of the legendary Montezuma, the Spaniards first tasted the delicious frothy drink prepared from the cocoa bean. The Aztecs served Montezuma his 'xocoatl' with great reverence before he visited his wives. Stout Cortés and his conquistadors killed Montezuma, conquered his kingdom, swiped the cocoa beans and began a century long Spanish monopoly of chocolate. Thomas Gage, the first Englishman to try it in 1648, didn't think much of it, calling it 'a spicy, scummy drink'.

Herbalists do not regard chocolate as a health drink but it does contain protein, carbohydrate, calcium, iron, vitamin A and several other aids to instant energy. In the eighteenth century it was declared 'a veritable balm of the mouth, for the maintaining of all glands and humours in a good state of health. Thus it is that all who drink it possess a sweet breath'. Casanova was among those who believed chocolate to be an aphrodisiac.

INGREDIENTS FOR TWO

100g (4oz) plain or bitter chocolate

600 ml (1 pint) milk, skimmed if preferred

Grated zest of ½ orange

150ml (¼ pint) whipped cream (optional)

Sprinkling of cocoa powder or ginger

METHOD

Put broken chocolate in pan with milk and heat gently, stirring until the chocolate is dissolved. Do not boil. Add orange zest and stir for two minutes. Remove pan from heat and strain into mugs or bowls. Top with a spoonful of cream or just sprinkle on ginger to give extra bite.

RHUBARB TANGO

The much neglected, too little appreciated Chinese rhubarb plant came to England via Russia. It is the roots which contain the most valuable medicinal goodies. But the stalks are the tasty parts and provide enough gastric astringent for a brisk purge, and are helpful for liver complaints. Rhubarb makes a deliciously refreshing morning drink.

INGREDIENTS FOR TWO

450g (1lb) rhubarb stalks

450ml (¾ pint) water

Sugar to taste

METHOD

Strip off tough outer fibres and leaves of rhubarb. Chop into 2.5cm (1 inch) pieces and place in heavy-based pan with water and sugar. Heat gently for about 15 minutes or until fruit is soft. Strain off the warm juice to drink and use the fruit to make a crumble or fool.

COFFEE WITH

HOT MILK

Avoid the sort of coffee which prompted the old Punch cartoon 'Look here, steward, if this is coffee I want tea, but if this is tea then I wish for coffee'. Aim for a stimulating wit-sharpening cup which would meet with Alexander Pope's approval 'Coffee surely makes the politician wise. And see through all things with his half shut eyes'. This recipe is for the simplest jug technique, a well-tried method which brings out the full flavour of the coffee. For the best taste, freshly roast and grind your favourite beans and use filtered water in hard water areas. One cup of coffee contains as much caffeine as a can of cola. Avoid too much of either because caffeine is toxic. Decaffeinated coffee is now widely available.

Drinking your *café au lait* from bowls cools it a little quicker and allows you the sensual delight of breathing in the aroma as you warm your hands. But without the milk, many would still agree with one seventeenth century opinion that coffee was 'black as soote, and tasting not unlike it'.

INGREDIENTS FOR TWO

2 rounded tablespoons ground coffee

600ml (1 pint) water

450ml (¾ pint) milk, skimmed if preferred

METHOD

Put the coffee into a warmed jug. Boil water in kettle and leave for a minute before pouring over grounds. With finer grounds use less water. Stir, cover and leave for six minutes. Bring the milk to just below boiling point in pan or microwave. Pour into warmed jug. Plunge spoon into coffee to settle floating grounds. Strain coffee into bowls and add hot milk.

LEMON BARLEY
WATER

This is a refreshing drink which is a lot more than a protein source for invalids' diets. Think of all those Wimbledon tennis players who sip it between sets. Barley has the lowest calorie count of all grains so it is ideal for slimmers. Alison Uttley in her *Recipes from an Old Farmhouse* describes it being used eighty years ago in Derbyshire for colds, to slake thirsts at harvest time and even given to the horses for a treat.

It is usually drunk cold and can be stored, but the lemon scent is stronger and it is at its best when warm. The addition of stewed, strained raspberries brightens the colour of this drink.

INGREDIENTS FOR TWO

1 tablespoon flaked barley, rinsed and strained

Juice and rind of 1 lemon

600ml (1 pint) water

METHOD

Place barley, lemon rind and juice into jug. Pour on boiling water and leave covered for one hour. Strain through a fine sieve, pressing barley into sieve to extract all juice into mug or glass. Add honey, sugar and hot water to taste.

NUTTY MILK

A really invigorating drink to give you breakfast bounce. Sipping your Nutty Milk should stop the sufferings described by Lytton Strachey: 'The horror of getting up is unparalleled, and I am filled with amazement every morning when I find I have done it'.

The dates in this recipe are packed with minerals, valuable vitamins and natural sugars, while the nuts and seeds, combined with milk, provide protein as well as vitamins.

INGREDIENTS FOR TWO

6 dried dates

25g (1oz) ground sesame or sunflower seeds

50g (2oz) ground hazelnuts

300ml (½ pint) milk

2 teaspoons honey

METHOD

Liquidize all the ingredients and heat gently in pan. You may add more milk for a less robust breakfast.

ELEVENSES

Time for a little
something! Like Winnie the Pooh we often feel like a
mid-morning smackerel. So, when the feeling comes
upon you, treat your tastebuds to these deliciously
refreshing drinks.

LEMON BALM
TEA

Lemon, or sweet balm, grows so profusely in most gardens that you might be tempted to pull it up and plant something else. Don't! The leaves make lemony tasting carminative tea and are still about until November or when the first frosts bite. As the name suggests 'balm' calms you down. Indeed it used to be given to treat hysteria. Now herbalists consider it useful for soothing mild digestive disorders, and others also believe it to be an anti-depressant. It has diaphoretic properties so it helps sweat out fevers.

A slow potter down the garden path to pick a small bunch of the heart-shaped leaves provides just enough exercise to justify your sitting down to enjoy the tea.

INGREDIENTS FOR TWO

**3 teaspoons of lemon balm leaves
or 2 teaspoons dried leaves**

450ml (¾ pint) boiling water

METHOD

Remove thick stalks and rinse leaves before placing in warmed pot and pouring in boiled water. Cover and infuse for five to ten minutes before straining and drinking with perhaps a dash of clear honey. The dried variety gives a delightful display as the leaves gently unfurl in the hot water.

PARSLEY TEA

Full of minerals and vitamins, and with a sharp tangy taste, parsley tea makes a healthy mid-morning drink which leaves your mouth feeling pleasantly clean.

One advantage of herb teas is how many there are to choose from. Herbalists stress the importance of varying the teas you drink as too much of one kind may not be good for the system. Parsley is a diuretic (increases the flow of urine) and can be useful for those with rheumatic or arthritic conditions. Being alkaline, it is good for diabetics.

You may, like many others, prefer your parsley raw or agree with Odgen Nash who thought 'parsley is gharsley'. The flat leaved variety is now available in shops and as a tea I prefer it to the more crinkly type.

I prefer to use fresh parsley rather than dried which does not give such a nice flavour.

INGREDIENTS FOR TWO

50g (2oz) fresh parsley leaves

600ml (1 pint) boiling water

METHOD

Rinse the parsley and bruise a little before placing it in a pot and pouring in boiled water. Cover and infuse for five minutes. Strain and pour into cups or glasses.

DANDELION
LEMON TEA

Try this for a change but don't drink too much. As its French name 'pissenlit' indicates dandelion leaves and roots are diuretic and can be used as a laxative. Herbalists suggest dandelions for many urinary conditions and even poor complexions and migraines. The leaves are plentifully available in French markets, mainly for use in salads, but are difficult to buy here. They are, however, easy to find in the wild although most gardeners would rather pull them out than cultivate them. Dandelion 'coffee' is made from the roots and is a more popular drink than the tea. Adding a little lemon makes the tea taste quite pleasant.

INGREDIENTS FOR TWO

**50g (2oz) fresh pale leaves, or two
teaspoons dried**

600ml (1 pint) boiling water

1 slice lemon

METHOD

Wash leaves. Place in warmed pot and
pour on boiled water. Infuse for five
minutes. Strain and serve with slice of
lemon and a dash of honey to taste. But
remember Henry Fielding's advice
that 'love and scandal are the best
sweeteners for tea'.

RUSSIAN TEA
WITH JAM

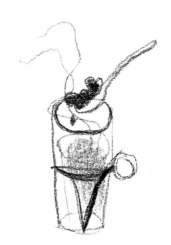

Traditionally Russian men drank their tea from glasses, and women from cups. According to Tolstoy, the samovar or urn was a 'sacred shrine' in the household. It was topped by a teapot with a strong infusion of tea to which boiled water from the tap below was added as required. Perhaps Mikhail Gorbachov's anti-vodka drive will increase tea drinking in the USSR which is already in the top four tea taking nations in the world. The British, of course, are top of the tea pops. Our most famous tea drinker was probably Dr Johnson who described himself a 'a hardened and shameless tea drinker who has for twenty years diluted his meals with only the infusion of this fascinating plant. Whose kettle has scarcely time to cool; who with tea amuses the evening, with tea solaces the midnight and with tea welcomes the morning'.

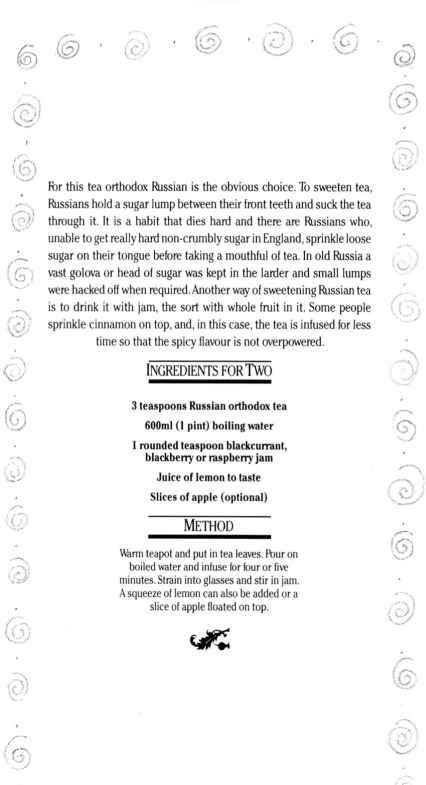

For this tea orthodox Russian is the obvious choice. To sweeten tea, Russians hold a sugar lump between their front teeth and suck the tea through it. It is a habit that dies hard and there are Russians who, unable to get really hard non-crumbly sugar in England, sprinkle loose sugar on their tongue before taking a mouthful of tea. In old Russia a vast golova or head of sugar was kept in the larder and small lumps were hacked off when required. Another way of sweetening Russian tea is to drink it with jam, the sort with whole fruit in it. Some people sprinkle cinnamon on top, and, in this case, the tea is infused for less time so that the spicy flavour is not overpowered.

INGREDIENTS FOR TWO

3 teaspoons Russian orthodox tea

600ml (1 pint) boiling water

**1 rounded teaspoon blackcurrant,
blackberry or raspberry jam**

Juice of lemon to taste

Slices of apple (optional)

METHOD

Warm teapot and put in tea leaves. Pour on boiled water and infuse for four or five minutes. Strain into glasses and stir in jam. A squeeze of lemon can also be added or a slice of apple floated on top.

LUNCH AND
PRE-PRANDIAL

If you find weekdays
or weekends spoiled by sleepy-making lunchtime
alcohol, or work at home and need an enlivening
drink, then these lunch and pre-prandial recipes, are
just the tonic you need. They can all be taken before
dining or just after lunch.

CHUNMEE
CHINA TEA

China is where cha all started; from the refined tea ceremony, now mainly restricted to Japan, to the grotesque habits of Samuel Johnson 'tearing his meat like a tiger and swallowing his tea in oceans'. The origin of tea, according to one legend, was the wise monk Bodhidharma who found he was becoming drowsy during meditation. He seized his offending eyelids, cut them off and threw them away. They took root and grew into a tea plant which makes the drink which drives away sleep.

The China Keemun teas are black and not astringent and said to be particularly suitable for those with weak digestions. Lapsang Suchong teas are noticeably tarry to taste. It is said their flavour originates from discarded fishermen's nets where the tea used to be dried. Lapsang Suchong is often mixed with other teas. These types of China tea are quite expensive so I have chosen a very refreshing and smooth green tea which can be drunk during a substantial meal. In *The Civilizing Influence of Tea* the author asks 'Is it going too far to inquire whether tea may not have borne an important part in the formation of that gentleness and tractability of character, which keeps the Chinese calm and orderly even in the midst of political revolutions?'

INGREDIENTS FOR ONE

1 teaspoon Chunmee China tea

Boiling water

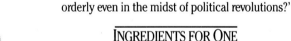

METHOD

Place tea in warmed teapot and pour on boiled water. Leave to brew for two minutes. Keep adding water as the tea becomes too strong. Some connoisseurs pour away the first cup of tea and concentrate on enjoying the second, less bitter infusion. The teapot remains on the table throughout the meal as the tea cleanses the palate between courses.

MANGO TEA

This is a great favourite among the increasingly popular combinations of fruit and flower teas. The fruit or flowers are added after the tea is processed so the petals or fruit are not singed. The best of these teas are made from good-quality large-leaf teas (often an Indian and China blend) to which the addition of mango flowers and oils gives a strong fruity scent and taste. There is none of the turpentine-like quality you can find in eating stringy unripe mangoes. Buddha himself rested in a mango grove, so you might find the tea really uplifting. A seventeenth-century traveller said of mangoes 'When ripe, the Apples of the Hesperides are but Fables to them; for taste the Nectarine, Peach and Apricot fall short'.

INGREDIENTS FOR ONE

1 teaspoon mango tea

300ml (½ pint) boiling water

METHOD

Place tea in a warmed bowl and pour on boiled water. Leave for two minutes while the leaves unfurl and sink to the bottom and then drink. Add more water when you reach near the leaves as the taste will otherwise become strong and bitter rather than light and naturally sweet as it should be.

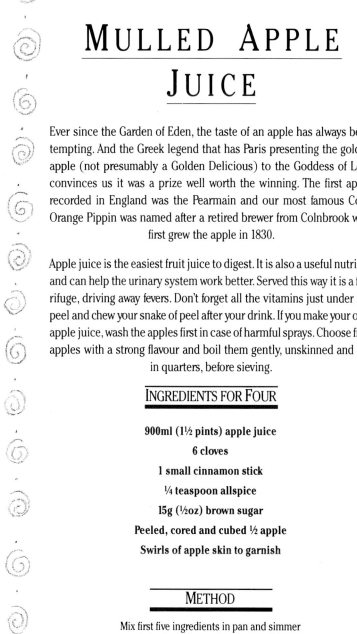

MULLED APPLE JUICE

Ever since the Garden of Eden, the taste of an apple has always been tempting. And the Greek legend that has Paris presenting the golden apple (not presumably a Golden Delicious) to the Goddess of Love convinces us it was a prize well worth the winning. The first apple recorded in England was the Pearmain and our most famous Cox's Orange Pippin was named after a retired brewer from Colnbrook who first grew the apple in 1830.

Apple juice is the easiest fruit juice to digest. It is also a useful nutrient and can help the urinary system work better. Served this way it is a febrifuge, driving away fevers. Don't forget all the vitamins just under the peel and chew your snake of peel after your drink. If you make your own apple juice, wash the apples first in case of harmful sprays. Choose firm apples with a strong flavour and boil them gently, unskinned and cut in quarters, before sieving.

INGREDIENTS FOR FOUR

900ml (1½ pints) apple juice

6 cloves

1 small cinnamon stick

¼ teaspoon allspice

15g (½oz) brown sugar

Peeled, cored and cubed ½ apple

Swirls of apple skin to garnish

METHOD

Mix first five ingredients in pan and simmer gently for five minutes. Leave to cool for an hour or so. Reheat carefully, add apple cubes, but do not let these become soggy. Serve in mugs or strong glasses garnished with snake of apple skin.

JAPANESE CHERRY TEA

An expensive tea but worth it for the gentle cherry aroma and flavour and the images of delicate Japanese painting that it conjures up. A good Japanese cherry tea is made of the unfermented green tea Sencha, to which natural essence of cherry is added. Sencha was first processed in the mid eighteenth century before which Matcha tea, the powdered type used in the tea ceremony, was used and only the ruling classes allowed to indulge. Sencha is carefully picked, carefully steamed so the colour remains and should be carefully and lovingly prepared. The Japanese consider that Sencha is best brewed at quite a low temperature (60° – 80°C) and is best made in a small earthenware pot. It can be served throughout a meal. Unlike black tea, however green tea contains vitamin C.

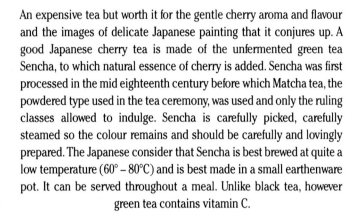

INGREDIENTS FOR TWO

1½ teaspoons Japanese cherry tea

450ml (¾ pint) water

METHOD

Place tea in warmed pot. Boil water and allow it to cool a little before pouring into pot. Leave to brew for no longer than two minutes or it will become bitter. Pour tea into delicate *little* bowls or cups. Do not fill bowl to top, so the rim can be held without burning your fingers. In Japan it is customary to make a slurping noise as you drink, particularly if the tea is hot.

TOMATO TREAT

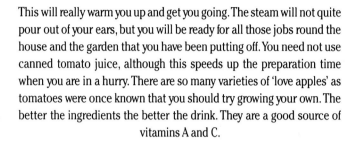

This will really warm you up and get you going. The steam will not quite pour out of your ears, but you will be ready for all those jobs round the house and the garden that you have been putting off. You need not use canned tomato juice, although this speeds up the preparation time when you are in a hurry. There are so many varieties of 'love apples' as tomatoes were once known that you should try growing your own. The better the ingredients the better the drink. They are a good source of vitamins A and C.

INGREDIENTS FOR ONE

1 small can tomato juice

150ml (¼ pint) water or to taste

Pinch of curry powder to taste

2 teaspoons lemon juice

METHOD

Heat the tomato juice and water in a saucepan,
stirring in the curry powder and adding the
lemon juice. Pour into glass with handle. If you
do not like curry powder, use a dash of
Worcester Sauce or Tabasco for this not too
Bloody Mary.

TEATIME

For most of us
teatime lacks the sparkling silver, paper-thin
cucumber sandwiches, and grace and dignity of
glorious empire days. But it can be great fun. For
those who like to exercise while they sip there are
still *thés dansants* taking place in different venues. In
London, there is a list of them, including the Ritz,
pinned up in the Tea House, Covent Garden. For those
with young children teatime is probably the happiest,
chattiest time of the day, especially if there is a new
drink to try. And for the sophistocats there are
special little whisks to buy to whip up tea at their own
tea ceremony. This does, however, take quite a time
to prepare.

HOT CHOCOLATE
WITH
MARSHMALLOW
ISLANDS

This drink is a great favourite with children, but they must promise extra toothbrush work afterwards. Before the passion for coffee swept France, drinking chocolate, believed by some to be an aphrodisiac, was the rage, particularly in court circles. The tall pots for chocolate were often silver with a small heater beneath or they were made in exquisite Sèvres china like Madame de Pompadour's. In his *A Tale of Two Cities* Dickens describes the decadent Monseigneur taking his morning chocolate. 'One lackey carried the chocolate pot into the sacred presence; a second mixed and frothed the chocolate with a little instrument he bore for that function; a third presented the favoured napkin; a fourth... poured the chocolate out.' The gastronome, Brillat Savarin, considered chocolate a drink 'most suitable for those who have much brain work; for clergymen, lawyers and above all, travellers'. In England the actor, David Garrick, adored chocolate grog and the Garrick Club served it at the bicentenary of his death. Helge Rubenstein, in her splendid *The Chocolate Book*, has a recipe for coffee and chocolate called 'Happy Marriage'. Mine is for less sophisticated palates.

INGREDIENTS FOR THREE

6 teaspoons chocolate powder

900ml (1½ pints) milk

1 packet *small* marshmallows

METHOD

Heat the milk to just below boiling point. Pour into mugs. Add two teaspoons (to taste) of chocolate powder to each mug and stir or whisk in. Float a few small marshmallows on top of each drink.

TILLEUL OR LIME TEA

Tilleul or lime (linden) blossom is probably the most famous tisane on the market. It is very popular in France where it is drunk after meals. Hercule Poirot took a tisane regularly, so perhaps it really is good for the little grey cells. It makes a perfect afternoon tea accompanied by madeleines, those small sponge cakes with a delicate vanilla flavour which so stirred the memory of writer Marcel Proust. His aunt used to dip the madeleines in her tisane and then hand them to the young Proust. Little did she know the effect on her nephew!

Lime trees blossom in June and July and can perfume a whole street. The flowers are dried until brittle and stored in plastic or paper bags. The scented flowers attract bees and have a honey-like smell. The tea used to be given to sweat out fevers and, even now, some people use it for its claimed medical properties as well as the sheer delight of the taste. It is used to clear coughs and colds, relieve fatigue, help indigestion and clear nervous headaches or migraines. It is also used to help the sleepless at bedtime, and some claim it strengthens the eye muscles. During the Second World War doctors prescribed this tisane as a tranquillizer for its sedative powers.

INGREDIENTS FOR TWO

**2 teaspoons dried lime flowers or
3 teaspoons fresh**

600ml (1 pint) boiling water

METHOD

Pour boiled water into warmed jug containing
flowers. Leave for four or five minutes then strain
into small cups or glasses.

INDIAN HOT
SPICED TEA

In India tea is often drunk during the day with samosas or cashew nuts. British visitors to India are often surprised to find milk and what seems to be a great quantity of sugar being boiled up with the tea. It can also be served without milk but with a slice of orange in it. Although tea is indigenous to the Assam region, the first teas grown there for commerce were from Chinese cuttings. British trade with India started in the 1840s. Pungent cardamom pods can also be used to reduce the bitter taste of coffee and are the special flavour of real Danish pastries. The Vikings probably brought them home from their travels. This spiced tea is particularly invigorating after a Sunday afternoon walk.

INGREDIENTS FOR SIX

1.15 litres (2 pints) water

½ stick cinnamon

4 cloves

4 cardamom pods, preferably green

**6 teaspoons black tea, a gutsy Ceylon or
strong Assam**

150ml (¼ pint) orange juice

Juice of 1 lemon

4 teaspoons sugar

Cinnamon sticks to serve

METHOD

Place spices in pan, cover with water, leave for five minutes and then bring to the boil. Pour over the tea and leave to brew for five minutes. Stir and pour through sieve on to sugar. Add orange juice and lemon juice and warm again without boiling. Serve with cinnamon sticks for stirring.

JAPANESE TEA

The tea ceremony started as a Zen Buddhist ritual in China where the tea's medicinal value was its virtue and the items used for the ceremony (kettle, water jar etc.) were placed on various shelves, the lowest one representing earth, the highest heaven. When Buddhism and Chinese influence came to Japan in about 710 AD, the once religious ritual became social. The powdered Matcha tea is presented to guests in an atmosphere of the utmost refinement and harmony in the tea room, 'an oasis in the dreary waste of existence'. All the senses and the mind should be purified and Teaism dictates that, on entering the tea room, one should have a clean face, clean hands and a clean heart. Gossip and politics are forbidden in conversation. Artwork on display and flowers in a vase should unite in tranquillity.

Among the Japanese teas available are Bancha, a coarse-grade green tea made from old brittle leaves and twigs, Sencha and Gen mai cha, a tea which contains toasted rice as well as pleasant tasting sencha. The rice floats on the surface and the leaves sit bright green in the depths of the bowl. I enjoy the nutty taste of the rice grains which reduce the tea's astringency. There is less tannin in green teas, some vitamin C and, because they are drunk lightly brewed, less caffeine.

INGREDIENTS FOR TWO

1½ teaspoons Sencha

600ml (1 pint) very hot water

METHOD

Shortly after it has boiled, pour water over leaves
in attractive bowls. I prefer white bowls which
show the pale green tea clearly. Leave for two
minutes and then drink. When the level is too
close to the leaves add more water. Do not
overfill bowls, so that your fingers can keep cool
on rim.

BERGAMOT TEA

The Red Indians were said to have taught the American settlers the benefits of this pleasantly scented tea known to them as Oswego. It was used as a remedy for chesty coughs and sore throats and said to ease headaches and cure nausea. One variety of bergamot provides the oil that flavours Earl Grey tea, but for tea-drinking purposes we use a different kind, easily grown in the garden, colourful and a great attraction to bees. To introduce yourself gently to a new herb infusion, it is a good idea to mix equal amounts of the new herb with an established favourite. You can gently accustom yourself to the scent of bergamot by pouring the tea into a hot revitalising bath.

INGREDIENTS FOR TWO

**2 teaspoons dried bergamot, or
5 teaspoons fresh**

600ml (1 pint) boiling water

Orange flower water (optional)

METHOD

Place the bergamot in a warmed pot.
Pour in the boiled water and infuse for
three minutes then strain, leave for a
little longer with fresh leaves. A little
orange flower water may be added.

JASMINE TEA

This refreshing contrast to hot chocolate evokes Shakespeare's warning: 'A surfeit of the sweetest things the deepest loathing to the stomach brings'.

Flavoured teas are not a new idea. In the eighteenth century ingredients were added to disguise the awful taste of cheap tea. Indeed an Act of Parliament was passed to stop 'smouch' which was made of dried and curled ash leaves then mixed with real tea and sold more cheaply. It was condemned for 'the ruin of fair trade' and 'the destruction of great quantities of timber woods and underwoods'. Tea was also made of old tea leaves coated in lead (black tea) or covered in verdigris (green tea).

The Chinese enhance their teas with rose petals or jasmine flowers. Try blending your own using a Ceylon or Darjeeling and adding a few petals of jasmine. Jasmine tea may be drunk on its own if you like neither Indian nor China tea. It has no real herbal properties but as a drink it is an exotic delight. Inhaled, jasmine oil is said to help meditation; in perfume it is used for sweetness and the flower can be crystallized.

INGREDIENTS FOR TWO

2 teaspoons good jasmine tea blend

600ml (1 pint) boiling water

METHOD

Pour boiled water on tea in warmed pot. Cover
and leave for three minutes. Serve. Do not
put too much scented tea in pot and avoid
leaving it to brew too long. It should have a
light taste.

EARLY EVENING AND SUPPER

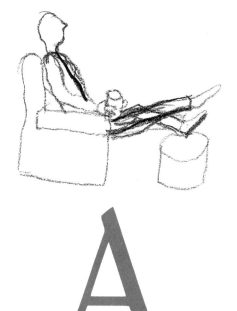

Aglass of wine or sherry can be a great unwinding temptation after a day's work, so in this section, I have made a long list of recommended alternatives to keep you from giving in. Spices or herbs will help ginger up bland fruit juices and teas, and tickle the most resistant palate. You can even enthuse about their bouquet, as long as it is a bouquet garni!

ALMOND FLIP

Almonds have a larger share of world trade than any other nut. They contain protein, iron and calcium and were adored by the Romans. It is said that sugared almonds (dragées) were distributed by a rich patrician family in Rome in 177 BC when there was a birth or a wedding in the family. They were extensively used by medieval cooks and transformed into marchpane (marzipan) for the Elizabethans. You might enjoy making your own salted almonds (frying blanched almonds in butter, draining and sprinkling with salt and cayenne pepper) to accompany this nutritious and aromatic drink.

INGREDIENTS FOR TWO

1 egg white

25g (1oz) ground almonds

25g (1oz) castor or icing sugar

One or two drops of almond essence

300ml (½ pint) milk

A pinch of nutmeg or ground cinnamon

METHOD

Whisk egg white until stiff, fold in almonds,
sugar and essence. Warm milk to just below
boiling point and fold in to mixture, or use
blender at a slow speed. Serve with ground
nutmeg or cinnamon sprinkled on top, in
strong glasses with handles.

GRAPEFRUIT
TODDY

A true Scottish toddy should contain spirits as well as sugar and water. The word comes from 'taudi' the Indian name for the sweet juice of the palm. The grapefruit is so called because it grows in grape-like clusters and began as a hybrid between the orange and the pomelo or shaddock in the West Indies. Grapefruits were still quite a novelty in the early part of this century and while some relished its health giving vitamin C others deplored the new habit of starting a meal with a grapefruit 'that parody of a lemon grafted on an anaemic orange'.

INGREDIENTS FOR TWO

**450ml (¾ pint) grapefruit juice
(use partly pink grapefruit for
colour and sweetness)**

2 or 3 cloves

Small cinnamon stick

Nutmeg (optional)

METHOD

Place all ingredients in pan and heat through.
Keep below simmering point for five minutes,
strain, serve with a sprinkling of nutmeg on top.

HIBISCUS PUNCH

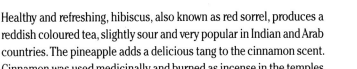

Healthy and refreshing, hibiscus, also known as red sorrel, produces a reddish coloured tea, slightly sour and very popular in Indian and Arab countries. The pineapple adds a delicious tang to the cinnamon scent. Cinnamon was used medicinally and burned as incense in the temples of ancient Egypt and used by the Romans for scented baths. In the middle ages cinnamon was used as an important ingredient in love potions. There's eugenol and the aldehyde cinnamol in the oil. The Aztecs believed vanilla, which contains vanillin, was good for the heart and protected against fevers. Vanilla is a marvellous seasoning which seems to extract the flavour it is mixed with. Always use pure essence or pod and avoid synthetic vanilla. The pod can be used several times before the flavour disappears.

INGREDIENTS FOR TWO

2 hibiscus tea-bags

Small vanilla pod

Juice and 2 chopped rings of pineapple

½ teaspoon ground cinnamon

600ml (1 pint) boiling water

1 tablespoon honey

METHOD

Place tea, vanilla, fruit and cinnamon in pan.
Cover with boiled water and lid and allow to
infuse for five or six minutes. Strain into
strong glasses or mugs and add honey to taste.

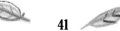

APRICOT GINGER

A pungent cocktail with plenty of healthy punch from the fruit juice and a hint of the exotic from the ginger. Apricots have a better flavour when dried than fresh, so I always keep a jar of them handy to nibble raw for their high potassium level. They also contain a hundred times more vitamin A than other fruit. I prefer the wrinkly, rather than the smooth, dried apricots.

INGREDIENTS FOR TWO

4 dried apricots, more if you enjoy their tang

300ml (½ pint) grapefruit juice, unsweetened

2 teaspoons honey

Sprinkling of ginger

METHOD

Soak apricots in water to cover until soft. Drain and mix with some of the grapefruit juice in a blender. Add remaining juice and honey and heat gently in pan. Do not boil. Add a little heated water if the cocktail is too strong and sprinkle ginger on top. Serve in strong glasses with handles.

GINGER PUNCH

Ginger was one of the first oriental spices to travel west and is now grown in Jamaica, West Africa and Central America, and Australia now produces an almost fibre-free ginger. The ancient Greeks enjoyed gingerbread and Pythagoras had a theorem that ginger plus gentian plus pepper plus honey equalled a cure for sickness. Ginger was probably brought to Britain by the Romans and became so popular in so many dishes that we now 'ginger up' ideas as well as meals.

INGREDIENTS FOR FIVE

50g (2oz) diced crystallized ginger

1 lemon

900ml (1½ pints) ginger ale

150ml (¼ pint) lemon squash

600ml (1 pint) water

50–75g (2–3oz) sugar

Grated nutmeg

METHOD

Put ginger and thinly sliced lemon into warmed punch bowl. Heat all other ingredients in pan and pour over ginger and lemon in punch bowl. Serve hot with grated nutmeg on top. For extra bite add 6 cloves and the peel of an orange and a lemon to the ingredients heated in the pan.

VEGETABLE JUICE
WARMER

Who knows, as a result of this substantial beverage you may develop W.S. Gilbert's 'sentimental passion of a vegetable fashion'. It might lead to your acquiring a taste for heated carrot or celery juice, more commonly drunk chilled. If you make a hot vegetable juice, don't let it become too thick and soupy and avoid too many root vegetables as they contain lots of starch which acts as a thickener. A few herbs, spices or a dash of Tabasco can pep up the taste of the blandest of vegetables. Heating vegetable juices destroys the vitamin B and C content, but vitamins A and D (fat soluble rather than water soluble) will not be lost if you microwave, steam or leave the lid on your pan when heating the vegetables.

INGREDIENTS FOR TWO OR THREE

3 sticks celery, washed and thinly sliced

50g (2oz) peas

350ml (12fl oz) tomato juice

4 tomatoes, skinned, seeded and chopped

2 spring onions, finely chopped

Salt and freshly ground black pepper

300ml (½ pint) chicken stock

2 tablespoons thick natural yoghurt

1 egg yolk

METHOD

Put all ingredients, except yoghurt and egg yolk, into saucepan. Bring to boil and simmer gently for six minutes. Blend in liquidiser or food processor. Mix yoghurt and egg together and add to vegetable juice. Heat gently and serve in strong glasses with handles or mugs.

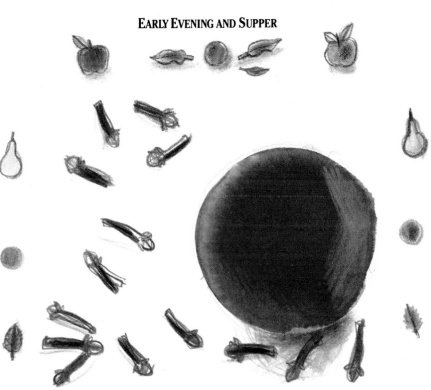

MOCK BISHOP

Real bishops are similar to the old wassail cups but they are never made with ale, usually it is port or claret. Now non-alcoholic wines are swelling supermarket shelves, so it is worth making a mock bishop. The drink was called bishop because of its purple colouring, and the clove-studded orange is known as a hedgehog.

INGREDIENTS FOR FOUR

1 bottle red non-alcoholic wine

1 orange

20 cloves

1 tablespoon sugar or honey
(optional)

METHOD

Stud the orange with cloves and bake in oven on tray for 30 minutes at 200°C/400°F/Gas 6. Cut baked orange into four segments and place with wine and sugar or honey (if required) in top of double boiler. Simmer for half an hour and ladle into strong glasses or mugs.

BEDTIME

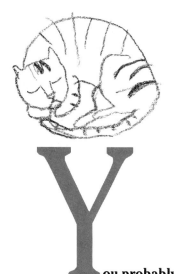

You probably already
have a favourite bedtime drink, the mere thought of
which conjures up comforting visions of a peaceful
end to the day. Certainly there are plenty of products
on the market offering bedtime comfort with the
promise of a good night's sleep. But how about a
change of approach! The best herbal tisanes for
helping sleep are camomile and lime flower. What
often keeps us awake is indigestion so camomile,
particularly the true camomile, *matricaria
chamomilla* with its ability to lessen stomach aches
and general restlessness, is probably the ideal. A cup
of this might be followed by a lavender bath: a strong
infusion of lavender tips poured into the bath water
to soothe your hyper-active brain.

CAROB WARMER

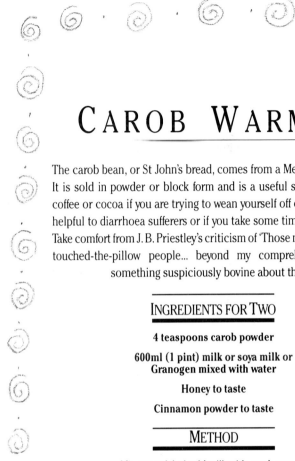

The carob bean, or St John's bread, comes from a Mediterranean tree. It is sold in powder or block form and is a useful substitute for tea, coffee or cocoa if you are trying to wean yourself off caffeine. It is also helpful to diarrhoea sufferers or if you take some time to get to sleep. Take comfort from J. B. Priestley's criticism of 'Those no-sooner-have-I-touched-the-pillow people... beyond my comprehension. There's something suspiciously bovine about them.'

INGREDIENTS FOR TWO

4 teaspoons carob powder

**600ml (1 pint) milk or soya milk or
Granogen mixed with water**

Honey to taste

Cinnamon powder to taste

METHOD

Mix spoonful of cold milk with carob powder until smooth. Bring rest of milk almost to the boil in pan and add carob mixture, stir and simmer. Serve in mugs with honey and sprinkling of cinnamon powder as required.

HONEY POSSET

A comforting drink to end the day and said to drive away colds. The Elizabethans drank their hot milk curdled with wine or ale, adding spices to taste. 'He goeth to bedde his posset smoaking hot,' *Man in the Moone*, 1600. Avoid the alcohol and you will have a nutritious and soothing beverage. If you are allergic to cow's milk or feel like a change try one of the substitute milks available in health shops. Do not try heating the powder type mixed with water because it tends to separate when hot. To curdle your posset, without using wine or ale, add the juice of half a lemon to the hot milk.

INGREDIENTS FOR TWO

4 teaspoons honey

2 glasses hot milk

Grated nutmeg or cinnamon to taste

METHOD

Stir the honey into the hot, not boiled, milk and serve in glasses or mugs with a sprinkling of nutmeg or cinnamon on the top. A posset can be made with malt extract instead of honey if you really need building up.

FLAKY MALTED
DRINK

This recipe is for microwave owners. Microwave cooking is a quick, economic way of heating drinks as you can heat the exact number you need. But do not overfill the mugs as the liquid may boil over the brim. As a drink, this is not recommended for slimmers but it makes a great reward after a trying day.

INGREDIENTS FOR ONE

300ml (½ pint) milk

2 teaspoons malted milk drink powder

1 large chocolate flake bar

1 tablespoon whipped cream (optional)

METHOD

Put milk in jug or mug. Microwave on high for two minutes. Stir in malted milk and break off quarter of flake and crumble into milk. Microwave on high for one minute. Place remaining flake in mug as a stirrer and float cream on top if you really want to let rip.

WHEAT GERM
POSSET

This is ideal for restoring the nerves after a hectic day. The germ (inner kernel) of the wheat contains vitamin E and some other vitamins, too. Both the germ and the bran are discarded in the making of white bread. So if you are a white bread addict this is your chance to get back some of those energising vitamins. Keep the wheat germ in the refrigerator as it perishes quite quickly. A posset used to be a hot milky drink curdled by adding wine or ale. It is much more satisfying made with honey and a sprinkling of cinnamon.

INGREDIENTS FOR ONE

1 tablespoon wheat germ

1 glass milk

1 teaspoon honey

Sprinkling of cinnamon

METHOD

Heat milk in pan to near boiling point. Remove from heat and stir in other ingredients. Serve in glass with holder or favourite mug. Sprinkle with cinnamon.

ROSEMARY TEA

'It tempteth, comforteth and saveth the brayne and all the heede' according to sixteenth century herbalist Richard Banckes. This tea is said to soothe you to sleep if you are nervous or suffer from cold feet. According to tradition, rosemary will not grow in an evil or unlucky person's garden. But you do not have to grow it, it is widely available in dried form. Ophelia thought of rosemary for remembrance and it is worth remembering to brew some before bed for rosemary 'suffreth not to dreeme fowle dreemes, not to be afeerde'. Its beneficial effect on the mind led ancient Greek students to wear sprigs of the aromatic herb in their hair to strengthen their memory.

As a tea it should relieve migraine and headaches, help indigestion problems and generally tone you up. Laboratory tests have shown that both thyme and rosemary have antiseptic properties so inhaling hot infusions of both with their volatile oils should help relieve asthmatic attacks. If you have trouble with your gums or bad breath, rosemary helps with that too. The tea has quite a bitter taste.

INGREDIENTS FOR TWO

2 teaspoons dried rosemary or 3 fresh

450ml (¾ pint) boiling water

Honey to taste

METHOD

Place dried or bruised fresh leaves in warmed teapot. Pour on boiled water. Cover and leave for up to ten minutes. Strain and serve, adding honey to taste.

COLD DAYS

I t can be difficult to be enthusiastic about taking a walk on a cold miserable day but do not be feeble hearted! A full thermos for company can transform a damp walk into an enjoyable adventure. Additions of cayenne, ginger or other hot spices to your favourite tea will stimulate the circulation and set your toes dancing in your wellington boots. A spiced tea is also invigorating if the central heating stops working in the office or if you feel guilty about turning the heating on earlier than usual when you are working at home.

APRICOT AND ORANGE SMASHER

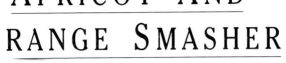

A delicious refreshing and low calorie drink which keeps well in a vacuum flask. Orange trees are very prolific which is why their blossom is an emblem of fecundity and is often worn by brides at their wedding. Being white the blossom also symbolises purity. If you have a sweet tooth mix a little honey with the smasher, or a sprinkling of cinnamon to pep up the circulation.

INGREDIENTS FOR FOUR

200ml (7 fluid oz) squeezed orange juice

25g (1 oz) dried apricots

Juice of ½ lemon

Cinnamon to taste

METHOD

Place apricots in a small pan and just cover with water. Simmer till soft. Add to fruit juices in blender and mix until thick and creamy. The smasher should be warm enough but if not add hot, boiled water to taste.

BUTTERSCOTCH BEAUTY

Children are particularly fond of this. In general they are happy with cold drinks as their circulation is in prime condition but Butterscotch Beauty is special. And it is even better for those who are older and whose circulation is slower. So gulp down this warming drink after a drenching walk in the rain.

INGREDIENTS FOR SIX

175g (6 oz) light brown sugar

150ml (¼ pint) hot water

1½ tablespoons butter or yellow fat

1.15 litres (2 pints) milk

Pinch of salt

1¾ teaspoons vanilla essence

Whipping cream and ground nutmeg to garnish

METHOD

Melt sugar over medium heat in large saucepan stirring constantly. Add hot water and bring to boiling point. Add butter or fat and cook for one or two minutes. Add milk and heat till hot but not boiling, stirring all the time. Blend in salt and vanilla essence. Serve garnished with whipped cream and ground nutmeg.

GINGER CORDIAL

A cheering beverage as its name suggests, invigorating to the heart and stimulating to the circulation. The addition of figs provides a certain laxative quality to the cordial but not enough to warrant rushing home early from a bracing walk. If you are trying this drink for the first time take pride in being a pioneer — remember Brillat Savarin: 'The discovery of a new dish does more for the happiness of mankind than the discovery of a star.'

INGREDIENTS FOR FOUR

225g (8 oz) figs or peaches, dried or fresh

½ teaspoon allspice

½ teaspoon ground ginger

¼ teaspoon ground cinnamon

¼ teaspoon mace or nutmeg

¼ teaspoon cloves

Cold water

600ml (1 pint) ginger ale

1 teaspoon cornflour

Few drops of lemon juice

METHOD

Stew fruit with spices and just enough water to cover. When soft, push through sieve or put in blender for thicker frothier effect. Return to pan with ginger ale and heat. Dissolve cornflour in small amount of water. Add this and lemon juice to taste, and seal in vacuum flask.

JAMAICAN
PINEAPPLE PUNCH

Usually served cold, this version will warm you up and start you thinking about the summer holidays. It's economical too as you can use up the pineapple peel you usually throw away.

INGREDIENTS FOR EIGHT

Peel of one large fresh pineapple

Peel of one orange

8 cloves

1 small cinnamon stick

50g (2oz) sugar

1.15 litres (2 pints) boiling water

150ml (¼ pint) fresh orange juice

150ml (¼ pint) fresh lemon juice

METHOD

Wash and peel pineapple and orange and place in large bowl with spices and sugar. Add boiling water, stir, cover and leave overnight. Reheat gently adding the fruit juices.

HOT SPICED ORANGE TEA

Four minutes is the right length of time to infuse this tea but some varieties require less. When in the seventeenth century tea first came to England one piece of advice from a Jesuit was 'The hot water should not stay upon the tea leaves any longer than you can say the Miserere Psalm very leisurely'. It's up to you!

INGREDIENTS FOR SIX

1.15 litres (2 pints) boiling water

50g (2oz) sugar

10 cloves

2 small cinnamon sticks

4 tea-bags (favourite blend)

4 tablespoons fresh orange juice

2½ tablespoons fresh lemon juice

Rind of ¼ orange

1 slice fresh lemon

6 long cinnamon sticks

METHOD

Combine water, sugar, cloves and cinnamon in saucepan. Mix and bring to boil. Remove from heat and add tea-bags. Infuse for four minutes. Strain and stir in remaining ingredients. Place over low heat to keep warm, do not boil. Discard orange peel. Serve in cups with long cinnamon sticks as mixers.

RHUBARB
CORDIAL

The Greeks called rhubarb *rha barbaron* as it arrived in Greece thanks to foreigners, barbarians. In fact it came from China but our present rhubarb is a pleasanter strain and can be delicious, particularly if you obtain the forced variety.

INGREDIENTS FOR FOUR

900g (2lb) rhubarb, chopped

25g (1oz) root ginger, chopped

100g (4oz) sugar

4 cloves

1.15 litres (2 pints) water

Orange slice or mint to garnish

METHOD

Gently simmer rhubarb and ginger with sugar, cloves and water until rhubarb is soft. Replace any liquid which has boiled away with more water. Strain and serve in warmed glass jug with sprig of mint or orange slice to decorate.

RUSSIAN
RASPBERRY

This is a great treat to return to after a long walk. If you cannot obtain fresh or frozen raspberries to extract their juice, use the syrup from the canned variety. If you grow raspberries in the garden (and they are an easy crop which, in wild form, even grows in Alaska) this is a good way of using up some of the less presentable berries.

INGREDIENTS FOR ONE

1½ tablespoons squeezed lemon juice

3 teaspoons raspberry juice

1 teaspoon icing sugar

Boiling water

Lemon slice for garnish

METHOD

Mix together fruit juices and sugar. Pour into glass or mug. Top with boiled water and garnish with a slice of lemon.

HOT DAYS

Forget the usual finger-tingling cold drinks clanking with ice and try a warm and equally thirst-quenching tea. This is so much less shocking for the system than cold meeting hot. You can have fun creating an elegant picnic in the garden or the park, setting out your best unchipped china. And if you are venturing farther afield, take a primus stove or vacuum flask and indulge in one of the following.

INDIAN TEA

One of the most delightful experiences of the summer is tea served in the open in your best porcelain cups. Sidney Smith sighed 'I am glad I was not born before tea'. And de Quincey in his *Confessions* claimed 'tea, though ridiculed by those who are naturally coarse, will always be the favourite beverage of the intellectual...' But possibly the most passionate tea bibber of all time was Gladstone who used to go to bed with a hot water bottle filled with tea.

I have chosen Darjeeling for this cuppa, the champagne of teas, delicate, with a bouquet reminiscent of muscatel. It is grown only in a small area of the Himalayas and should not be made with too many leaves because this makes it harsh and acidic. Some may prefer a richer tea like Assam. Unlike wine, which is made from annual grape picking, tea is picked daily, and varies considerably, and thus makes generalizations about quality difficult.

INGREDIENTS FOR TWO

3 teaspoons Darjeeling tea, choose a quality one with good large leaves

600ml (1 pint) boiling water

METHOD

Warm the teapot and put in tea leaves. Pour on water which has just boiled. Never let the water become over boiled as this spoils the taste and, according to experts, the smell. Brew for up to five minutes. Strain and serve, or seal in vacuum flask.

LEBANESE SPICE
TEA

Among the weeds growing in the Roman Forum are some with crescent moon shaped seeds. If you nibble these you will taste anise, a favourite flavouring and breath freshener among the ancient Romans. You have probably tried sprinkling these seeds over salads or for flavouring bread or cakes. Now's your chance to try them in tea.

INGREDIENTS FOR FOUR

1 tablespoon ground ginger

1 tablespoon caraway seeds

1 tablespoon anise seeds

Pinch of nutmeg

900ml (1½ pints) boiling water

4 whole almonds or walnuts

Honey

METHOD

Place all ingredients in pan except nuts and boil for five minutes. Place a nut in the bottom of each cup and strain on spiced tea. Sweeten to taste with honey.

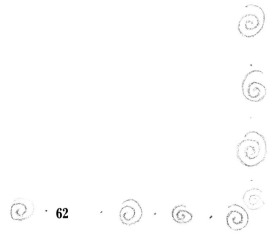

LEMON GRASS
TEA

Apart from peppermint, lemon grass, or citronella, is probably the best initiation into herbal tea rites. It has a sweet lemony flavour and if you find this overpowering try combining it with another herb. Nowadays no significant medicinal claims are made for it, but being rich in vitamin A it is reckoned to be beneficial to acne-sufferers in clearing the complexion. You can grow your own clump of pleasantly-scented lemon grass in a window-box or in a pot indoors.

INGREDIENTS FOR TWO

2 teaspoons dried lemon grass or 3 freshly chopped

600ml (1 pint) water

Lemon slice or sprig of mint for garnish

METHOD

Warm the pot and put in herbs. Pour in boiled water and infuse for three minutes. Strain into small cups garnished with a slice of lemon or sprig of mint.

MOROCCAN MINT TEA

Not a drink for anybody trying to cut down on sugar because they like their tea and coffee really sweet in Morocco. But the mint makes it a very refreshing drink. You can see the tiny glands that secrete mint's aromatic oils if you look closely at the leaves. They are the translucent dots. There is a belief that crushed mint left in a room drives away flies. I am sure that William Cobbett had not tasted this recipe when he advised young men to 'Free yourself from the slavery of tea and coffee and other slopkettle'.

INGREDIENTS FOR FOUR

3 teaspoons green tea

2 tablespoons sugar (or to taste)

1 tablespoon chopped fresh mint

600ml (1 pint) water

Ground pepper (optional)

METHOD

Place tea, sugar and mint in teapot. Pour in
boiling water and infuse for five minutes. Stir
and strain into glasses or small cups. Sprinkle
with pepper if you are feeling brave.

MEXICAN
GRANDMA

This is a marvellously refreshing drink. With its phosphates of magnesium, calcium and potassium the camomile has a soothing effect on the nerves and digestion. The fruit juices also supply a good quantity of vitamins. A tonic delight to sip as you sit outside enjoying the balmy days of summer.

INGREDIENTS FOR TWO

2 tea-bags camomile tea

450ml (¾ pint) boiling water

2 cloves

Juice of 1 orange and 1 lemon

2 teaspoons honey or to taste

**Orange or lemon slice or sprig of mint to
garnish**

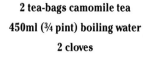

METHOD

Place tea-bags in a small pan, pour on boiled
water and leave, covered, to infuse for five
minutes. Remove tea-bags and add cloves,
fruit juices and honey to pan and reheat gently.
Remove cloves and pour into glasses with
holders. Serve with a slice of fruit on the side of
the glass or a sprig of mint on top.

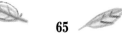

IN SICKNESS

We are all aware of the side effects (and inside effects) of some chemically manufactured drugs. So when you are suffering from a minor ailment, you may prefer to try these old favourites of re-discovered herbal teas. Use them in moderation and not in place of an important prescribed medication. For a long time, before imported tea became the soothing comforter for all classes, sage tea was the national beverage. Even if you are an inveterate tea drinker when you are well, your taste may turn to one of these infusions or remedies when you are feeling under the weather.

BEEF TEA

This old-fashioned beverage helps convalescents regain their appetites, and is particularly good for those unable to take solids. It was the tradition to serve the equivalent to beef tea to passengers on board ship as they crossed the equator on their return to England. It probably helped with seasickness in the Bay of Biscay, too. Easily digested, beef tea has a high nutritive value but chiefly it stimulates the appetite and the digestive glands. It was originally kept in hermetically sealed bottles. Mrs Beeton offers sensible advice to those feeding an invalid: 'Consult the patient as little as possible for a sick person should not be bothered about selecting dishes'. Concentrate on offering very small quantities — you can always give seconds — and present on an attractive tray with other nourishing temptations.

INGREDIENTS FOR THREE

450g (1lb) skirt of beef

600ml (1 pint) water

½ teaspoon salt

1 small sliced carrot

½ small sliced turnip

1 small sliced onion

Bouquet garni

METHOD

Remove fat from meat. Place in double saucepan, add water, salt and other ingredients. Simmer two or three hours, strain, cool and remove fat from surface. Reheat without boiling. Beef tea can also be cooked in a low oven 120–140°C/250–270°F/Gas ½–1 in a carefully sealed casserole for two or three hours. A beaten egg yolk can be stirred into the heated tea for added nourishment.

APPLE TEA

Both camomile and peppermint teas, with their beneficial effects on digestion, have already been mentioned. Apple tea, with its vitamins B and C, is said to help bladder trouble, supplying helpful nutrients to the urinary system. And if you are feverish, it is light and pleasant. So do not spurn those slightly wrinkled apples in the fruit bowl. Turn them into this appealing apple tea.

INGREDIENTS FOR ONE

4 apples, number will depend on juiciness and variety

Brown sugar to taste

Water to taste

METHOD

Carefully wash apples to remove any harmful spray. Slice whole, unpeeled apples into pan with very little water, cover and cook till soft. Keep peeping under lid to check the slices do not stick to the pan. Strain, serve and add brown sugar to taste and more boiled water if required. Apple tea can also be made using the skin of ripe, unblemished, apples steeped for just a few minutes in boiling water.

BORAGE LEAF TEA

Borage conjures up high summer days when it decorates glasses of Pimms with its hairy leaves and blue flowers. The tea however is much more beneficial: once regarded as an aphrodisiac, it is more usually rated as a tonic, an anti-depressant or, by Richard Mabey, as a cure for a hangover.

Herbalists advise borage tea to purify the system, dispel fevers, boost the heart and stimulate the adrenal glands. Its name in Celtic means 'man of courage' and it was said to give confidence to the timid — presumably before battle. Fresh leaves contain potassium and calcium and so are said to be handy for hysteria or a mild case of heart palpitations. There is less belief nowadays in its help for rheumatism sufferers but it is effective in soothing the effects of nasal catarrh.

Borage is easy to grow, much loved by bees, and the fresh leaves are infinitely preferable to dried ones. The taste is cucumber-like.

INGREDIENTS FOR TWO

50g (2oz) fresh borage leaves with flowers
600ml (1 pint) boiling water
Pinch of lavender flowers

METHOD

Pour boiled water into pot then add the bruised leaves. This avoids the bitterness which can occur when boiling water is poured on to the leaves. Cover and leave for ten to fifteen minutes. Strain and serve in small bowls so you can inhale the goodness at the same time as drinking. A pinch of lavender flowers gives this infusion an extra tonic effect.

ELDERFLOWER
TEA

Elder trees are widespread and spring up even in hedgerows and on waste land. They were believed to ward off witches. I love the particularly pungent scent of the flowers in June and often use a head of the flowers to flavour gooseberry crumbles and pies. In orthodox medicine the flowers are used to make up skin and eye ointments. Herbalists recommend elderflower tea for those with catarrh and colds. Snuffle-stricken children particularly benefit from a small cup of elderflower tea with a few leaves of mint added and a little honey. It was Ogden Nash who noticed that 'some girls with a snuffle their tempers are uffle'. And this is the remedy to change them to the ideal child who is 'snivelly civilly'. Enthusiasts claim a cupful of this infusion before breakfast does wonders for their bodily and mental health. The tea is also meant to help sufferers from hay fever.

INGREDIENTS FOR TWO

**25g (1oz) elderflowers, dried or fresh,
dried taste stronger but have less scent**

600ml (1 pint) water

Honey to taste

METHOD

Bring saucepan of water to the boil, add
flowers, cover and simmer for one minute.
Leave tea to sit another minute, then strain into
small cups. Any elderflower tea left over can be
used as an astringent skin wash.

E GG N OG

Egg nog or egg flip sounds like an expletive or a children's comic character but it is, in fact, an extremely nourishing hot drink. Especially if you are not feeling well enough to cook a proper meal. Think of all the protein and calcium in this recipe. Soya milk can be used instead of cow's milk.

INGREDIENTS FOR TWO

450ml (¾ pint) milk

2 teaspoons honey

Few drops vanilla essence

2 eggs

A little cream (optional)

Grated nutmeg or ginger to taste

Pinch of coriander or elderflower (optional)

METHOD

Warm the milk in pan but do not boil. Stir in honey and vanilla. Place eggs in blender or beat by hand in jug and then gradually add the warm milk. Serve in glass or mug with a little whipped cream and a sprinkling of nutmeg on top. Some people prefer to flavour their egg nog with coriander or elderflower mixed in with hot milk.

RASPBERRY LEAF TEA

Raspberry leaf tea is available in packet form from health shops but freshly picked leaves are much better. Wild raspberries grow abundantly in woodland but you may need Richard Mabey's *Food for Free* to distinguish them from wild unripe blackberries. A pleasant drink can be made from the berries themselves but it is the astringent leaves, high in vitamin C, which make the tea so beneficial for expectant mothers. If it is taken daily from about the sixth month of pregnancy it is thought to ease childbirth and the expulsion of the afterbirth. Lactation is also helped and, as it tones up the mucous membranes, it is good after childbirth to encourage bowel action and strengthen other tired muscles. The recommended quantity is a cupful drunk warm, two to three times a day. This tea can help relieve colds and drive away premenstrual cramps and heaviness. If you are pregnant, it would be wise to consult a herbal practitioner before starting a course of Raspberry Leaf tea.

INGREDIENTS FOR TWO

**25g (1oz) dried or 50g (2oz) fresh
raspberry leaves, chopped**

600ml (1 pint) water

Honey to taste

Lemon juice (optional)

METHOD

Pour boiled water over leaves in warmed pot and leave to brew for three minutes (some experts say ten). Strain and serve with honey to sweeten and a squeeze of lemon juice to taste.

FENNEL SEED TEA

The Reverend Sidney Smith might have been thinking of this tea when he said, 'I am convinced digestion is the great secret of life'. For fennel eases indigestion, gets rid of wind and helps you pass water. A warm teaspoonful is recommended for colic ridden babies. Some dislike the aniseed taste of fennel, dill and caraway and obtain similar results from camomile, peppermint and balm teas. Fennel seed tea stimulates the milk flow of breast feeding mothers and counters post natal depression. Any tea left over and cooled can be used to bathe sore eyes and make them sparkle. Fennel has been used by herbalists for centuries:

> 'In Fennel-seed, this vertue you shall find
> Foorth of your lower parts to drive the winde
> Of Fennel vertues foure they do recite
> First it hath power some poysons to expell
> Next, burning Agues will it put to flight,
> The stomack it doth cleanse, and comfort well;
> And fourthly, it doth keepe and cleanse the sight
> And thus the seede and herbe doth both excell'.

The Englishman's Doctor 1608

INGREDIENTS FOR ONE

2 teaspoons crushed or ground fennel seed

600ml (1 pint) boiling water

METHOD

Crush seed with a teaspoon and put in warmed teapot. Pour on boiled water, cover pot with tea cosy and leave to infuse for ten minutes. Strain and serve a little at a time. Wash teapot carefully. Tea can also be made with the leaves of fennel, but this is medicinally less good.

SAGE TEA

As its name suggests, sage tea is the wisest choice. *Salvia*, its Latin name, means to heal or save and its medicinal powers have been recognised since the time of the ancient Egyptians. The claims of its powers are legion. It makes your life longer, your memory sharper and keeps your liver and your nerves in perfect working order. Sage has anti-inflammatory properties and restricts bacteria growth. It is meant to stop sweating. It also has the power of 'dispelling of evil spyrites'. Alison Uttley, who wrote *Little Grey Rabbit*, remembers being given sage tea as a child to relieve colds.

If you grow your own sage, pick the leaves in spring before the bush flowers and dry in paper bags in an airy place.

INGREDIENTS FOR ONE

1 teaspoon dried sage or 2 fresh or 1 tea-bag

300ml (½ pint) boiling water

Squeeze of lemon or orange juice

METHOD

Place leaves in a warmed infuser or mug, if using teapot clean thoroughly afterwards. Pour on boiled water and cover to prevent volatile oils with their therapeutic qualities evaporating. Leave for from three to ten minutes. Strain and add a squeeze of orange or lemon. Any sage tea left over can be dabbed on insect bites to stop itching and stinging.

ROOIBOSCH TEA

Translated as red bush tea and grown in the Cape Province of South Africa, it is available in sachets from health shops. Rooibosch tastes very like real tea and contains less tannin and lots of vitamin C. Many claims have been made about its curative powers and it is certainly prescribed by herbalists for those with digestive problems. Rooibosch has a great advantage over other herbal teas which is that it can be served with milk, and milk is undoubtedly a quick way of cooling tea to the required temperature. Most herbal teas do not take milk.

INGREDIENTS FOR TWO

2 sachets Rooibosch

600ml (1 pint) boiling water

Milk (optional)

Sugar (optional)

METHOD

Pour the boiled water over the sachets in a warmed teapot. Infuse for five minutes. Serve with or without milk and sugar.

IN HEALTH

If you are feeling
fighting fit, this is the perfect time to be adventurous
and test your palate with unexpected tastes that can
enliven you even more to face any foe, climb every
mountain and tackle that task or phone call that you
have been putting off. But remember, moderation in
all things. As Anacharsis, the Scythian philosopher,
said, drink 'the first cup for thirst, the second for
pleasure' and avoid 'the third for intemperance'. An
even stronger warning came from George Herbert:
'Drink not the third glass — which thou canst not
tame when once it is within thee'.

American Spiced Punch

Allspice, one of the ingredients in this delicious party drink, is the spice Columbus missed. He sailed twice past the Caribbean islands in search of spices and gold and failed to notice the potential value of the allspice trees, probably because the fruit were not yet ripe. Pirates used allspice to preserve their meat and called it boucan – hence they were called boucaneers or buccaneers.

Ingredients for Twelve

100g (4oz) sugar

300ml (½ pint) water

2 small cinnamon sticks

1 teaspoon chopped ginger

½ teaspoon cloves

½ teaspoon whole allspice

150ml (¼ pint) fresh lemon juice

600ml (1 pint) fresh pineapple juice

450ml (¾ pint) fresh grapefruit juice

300ml (½ pint) apricot nectar

Fresh orange slices cut in half and studded with cloves to garnish

Method

Place sugar, water, cinnamon in saucepan. Put ginger, cloves, allspice in tea ball or muslin bag and add. Bring to boil for five minutes. Remove spices and add fruit juices. Heat to just below boiling point. Serve in mugs or punch cups with orange slices studded with cloves floating on top.

CARAWAY TEA

An excellent digestif after a large meal — the liqueur kümmel is made of caraway. The seeds contain essential oils, proteins, sugar and pentosans and are alleged to prevent belching and other wind problems. The Roman writer, Pliny, believed caraway was good for pallid complexions. As it is an appetite stimulant a glass before a dinner party might give you the glow you lack.

INGREDIENTS FOR ONE

1 teaspoon caraway seeds, or less for your first try

300ml (½ pint) boiling water

METHOD

Crush the seeds in the warmed teapot – this stops them flying all over the chopping board and pour on the boiled water. Leave covered for several hours. Reheat, strain and serve.

ARAB COFFEE

Just as the Japanese have a tea ceremony, so the Arabs have a coffee ceremony with the most favoured guest sitting on a mat nearest the fire. Coffee is, of course, very important in Moslem countries where alcoholic drinks are not permitted. To avoid caffeine many people nowadays use decaffeinated beans or even dandelion root coffee (easily obtained from health shops and good for rheumatism). There are claims that coffee can actually be beneficial: it is said to cure cold sores if dabbed on the affected area, and it was the unusual friskiness of Kaldi's goats in Arab legend which is said to have led to the discovery of the first coffee plant upon which the goats had been feeding.

INGREDIENTS FOR TWO

2 split cardamom pods

4 heaped teaspoons pulverized coffee (high roast)

2 heaped teaspoons sugar

600ml (1 pint) water

1 teaspoon ground ginger

METHOD

Add the pods, coffee and sugar to the water and gently simmer for about twenty minutes or try the nerve racking process of heating the coffee in small pan or proper jazoua, removing from the heat three times after it foams up. To help the grounds settle, the teaspoonful of ground ginger can be added.

GINSENG TEA

An oriental cure all, Ginseng, or the root of life is said to rejuvenate and cure impotence. Some people claim their daily dose of ginseng has given them a new lease of life but there are plenty of sceptics. It takes six years for the root to grow to suitable proportions for picking which accounts for the expense of the tea-bags which come from Korea and the USA. The ground and dried root contains many organic acids, minerals enzymes and vitamins and has its principal effect on the pituitary gland. So solid, placid individuals are said to benefit from the zip a cup of ginseng brings, but normally hyperactive types should perhaps avoid it. As it is so expensive it may be worth first trying one of the Japanese mixtures of ginseng with other plants, such as peony, which are widely available from health shops.

INGREDIENTS FOR ONE

1 ginseng tea-bag
150ml (¼ pint) water

METHOD

Follow advice on the packet or add near boiling
water to the tea in warmed pot. Infuse for
three to five minutes and serve in a cup or bowl.

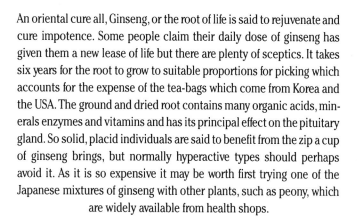
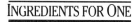

GINGER TEA

To keep you awake, ginger has few peers. The knobbly rhizomes of ginger are now easily available at supermarkets and greengrocers. They keep well so, rather than a good quality powder, grate a root yourself. Roots are sometimes called races or hands. Grated ginger in hot camomile tea is said to cure travel sickness, so take a vacuum flask of it on long journeys. A spoonful of honey enhances it. The carminative (digestion helping and flatulence dispelling) effects of ginger are recognized and the tang alone certainly counteracts drowsiness. In Lebanon, spiced teas are served in a cup with a whole almond or walnut in the bottom, a delightful treat to chew after the spicy tea.

INGREDIENTS FOR TWO

2 teaspoons or 15g (½oz) grated ginger

2 teaspoons anise or caraway seeds

2 favourite blend tea-bags

300ml (½ pint) boiling water

Honey to taste or pinch or nutmeg

METHOD

Pour boiled water over spices and tea-bags in a
small pan and leave for four minutes before
serving. For a richer taste, simmer the spices
for five minutes before adding tea-bags.
Sip a little at a time with a drop of honey
or a sprinkling of nutmeg.

ODDBALL

These might amuse
you and any guests who may be on the wagon.
Non-alcoholic drinks have the advantage that you can
enjoy them at any time of day. There is no need to wait
until six o'clock in the evening, no need to worry that
after your Mock Bishop or Negus you will work less
efficiently. Neither your motor functions nor your
little grey cells will be impaired. The drinks taste
good too but there is one disadvantage noticed by a
French gastronome (obviously not a medical man)
who complained 'that the neck is, from its shortness
a hindrance to the pleasure of tasting'.

YERBA MATÉ

This is a stimulating beverage made from the crushed or powdered leaves of Ilex Paraguayensis and is available from health shops. Widely drunk in Argentina, Paraguay, Uruguay and Brazil, maté is named after the special hollowed gourds it is served in. These are silver edged and can be worn slung from a belt. The tea is sipped up through a silver tube or straw and tastes like a slightly smoky Indian tea. Maté is often used as a tonic to liven up the mind and is recommended to students busy with revision. Slimmers, too, are advised to make up some maté rather than eating between meals.

INGREDIENTS FOR TWO

2 tablespoons maté

600ml (1 pint) boiling water

Sugar and milk (optional)

METHOD

Add maté to the warmed teapot. Pour in boiled or just boiling water and allow to steep for five to ten minutes. Serve in small cups.

NEGUS

Originally Colonel Francis Negus concocted the sweet spiced wine for George I. The difference between a negus and a mulled wine is the method of heating: to mull a wine you stick in a hot poker or warm it in a pan. To make a negus you add hot water. If you prefer to serve a stronger concoction resembling a mulled wine, simmer the ingredients below in a pan without the water, adding more spices and the peel of an orange and a lemon.

INGREDIENTS FOR TWELVE

1 bottle non-alcoholic wine – available from most supermarkets

300ml (½ pint) soda water or sparkling water

1 small cinnamon stick

6 cloves

12 slices lemon

2.25 litres (2 quarts) boiling water or to taste

Grated nutmeg to garnish

METHOD

Mix all ingredients in jug or bowl. Serve in mugs or strong glasses and sprinkle with nutmeg.

PARTY PUNCH

This pleasant fruity punch is pretty to look at and will not give a hangover requiring a peppermint or lavender tea cure. Sachets of spices can be found in shops in the UK but the best are obtained from Austria or Switzerland where they dunk the sachets into individual glasses of hot wine and water. I find the two spices used here quite pungent enough particularly if the punch is to be served at a teenagers' party. This is perfect too for those who agree with Othello, 'I have very poor and unhappy brains for drinking. I could well wish courtesy would invent some other custom of entertainment.'

INGREDIENTS FOR EIGHT

2–3 tablespoons brown sugar or honey to taste

6 tablespoons fresh orange juice

3 tablespoons lemon juice

900ml (1½ pints) apple juice

12 cloves

2.5cm (2 inch cinnamon stick)

1 tablespoon cherry juice

1 sliced lemon

1 sliced apple

Zest of ½ orange

METHOD

Dissolve sugar in orange, lemon and apple juice. Add cloves, cinnamon and cherry juice, heating slowly to below boiling point. Remove from heat and leave for two hours to infuse. Reheat carefully without boiling, add lemon and apple slices and orange zest. Serve in warmed tankards, strong glasses or mugs.

KASHMIRI TEA

International food writer, David Scott, has devised this 'approximation' of the sweet tea drunk in Kashmir. Other recipes include more cardamom pods and almonds and combine the tea leaves together in an infusion before straining the boiled spices into the pot with them. The milk can be reduced in quantity and added cold to the cups, but in this case, double the amount of water.

INGREDIENTS FOR FOUR

600ml (1 pint) milk

600ml (1 pint) water

3 teaspoons green tea

6 cardamom pods, crushed

6 blanched chopped almonds

1 teaspoon pine nuts

2 cloves

¼ teaspoon cinnamon

METHOD

Simmer all ingredients for 15 minutes. Strain.
Add more boiling water if the tea is too reduced.
To be truly exotic, add a pinch of saffron to the
cup for its scent.

PEPPERMINT PUFF

Not a good idea for slimmers, but heavenly for those with a sweet tooth who are trying to avoid those sticky post-prandial liqueurs. It might make a pleasant stirrup cup for a departing guest who is about to brave the gusting elements by horse, or, more likely, for the guest being thrust into his wellington boots for a cold walk home.

INGREDIENTS FOR ONE

2 peppermint creams or a few drops of peppermint essence

2 marshmallows

300ml (½ pint) hot, not boiling, milk

METHOD

Dissolve peppermint and marshmallows in milk. Whisk in blender until frothy, serve in a mug and drink before it cools.

QUICK CARDAMOM COFFEE

A delicious treat to offer guests who pop in after dinner. It is quickly made in a microwave. Although instant coffee and coffee essence are not rated as coffee by some connoisseurs, they are useful for achieving a coffee flavour quickly. Real coffee can, of course, be substituted. Napoleon was a keen coffee drinker and declared 'It gives me a pain that is not without pleasure. I would rather suffer than be senseless'.

INGREDIENTS FOR ONE

150ml (¼ pint) milk

150ml (¼ pint) water

1 tablespoon coffee essence

1 or 2 crushed cardamom pods

1 tablespoon whipped cream

METHOD

Pour milk and water into a jug. Stir in coffee essence and add cardamom. Microwave on high for three minutes. Strain into mug and blob cream on top.

DUTCH CHRISTMAS TREAT

A filling drink to be enjoyed by adults and children on Christmas Eve.
You could even leave a mug for St. Nicholas.

INGREDIENTS FOR TWO

1 small cinnamon stick

4 cloves

¼ teaspoon saffron

1 small flake of mace

4cm (1½ in) chunk ginger root

300ml (½ pint) milk

1 tablespoon sugar

3 teaspoons cornflour

2 teaspoons cold water

METHOD

Tie spices in muslin bag and place with milk
in saucepan. Bring to just below boiling
point and simmer for 15 minutes. Add sugar
with cornflour dissolved in water. Simmer
for five more minutes. Remove muslin bag
and serve hot in mugs.

GROW YOUR OWN
HERBS

Most garden centres have a wide selection of herbs for you to grow from seed or seedlings. The National Centre for Organic Gardening, Ryton-on-Dunsmore, Coventry CV8 3LG produces an excellent catalogue which includes many herbs.

Most herbs are happy in a light soil, so avoid fertilizer but remember to water them. Plant your herb garden as near your kitchen door as possible so you can reach it easily whatever the weather. You can arrange the different plants in Elizabethan knot garden formation, small beds surrounded and joined together by low, neat hedges in the form of lovers' knots, in segments of a circle or as a rockery, but do not crowd them, particularly mints which are prone to rust disease. If planted too close to each other dill and fennel lose their individual flavour. Parsley prefers a lusher, heavier soil than most other herbs.

An attractive assortment of herbs can also be grown in terracotta containers or strawberry jars, window boxes or in individual pots indoors. If using one container for several herbs avoid mint with its rampant roots — give it a special pot instead. Herbs grown indoors tend to be straggly or stunted, but a good mix of shop-bought soil and a thorough weekly soak can produce a regular supply of herbs for making drinks and for cooking as well as fragrance.

DRY YOUR OWN HERBS

Herbs should be cut with scissors in the early morning once the dew has evaporated. They are best picked before they come into flower when the flavour of the herbs will be at its strongest. Do not pick diseased plants.

Clean the herbs before drying thoroughly, out of direct sunlight; sunlight will remove the essential oils. Either hang the herbs, tied with raffia or thin string, upside down in a warm place or spread in thin layers on racks covered with newspaper in a room where dry air circulates gently. This process should take about a week, but be patient or the herbs may go mouldy later on. Finish with a short warm up, for the herbs, in a moderate oven.

A quicker way of drying herbs is to use a microwave oven. Place herbs on absorbent paper in an oven-proof dish and turn microwave to maximum. Leave for three minutes or until brittle. Some herbs take less time — Chervil, for example, only one or two minutes, so it is worth checking progress every 30 seconds or so after the first minute. Leave herbs for two hours before placing in airtight jars. One advantage of the microwave system is that it preserves the colour of the herb, particularly noticeable with parsley.

Store your herbs in airtight jars out of direct sunlight, removing the larger stalks of plants like mint and lightly crumbling the whole of small-leaved herbs like thyme.

WHERE TO DRINK TEA

Betty's, 188 High Street, Northallerton, Yorkshire provides a wide variety of teas to drink from fine bone china and serves home-made scones and cakes. There are other Betty's in Harrogate, York and Ilkley, but it is the Northallerton tea-shop which won the Top Tea Place of the Year Gold Award (1987) chosen by the Tea Council. Betty's also sells tea at its various branches.

The Best Cuppa award (1987) given by the Tea Council and the *South Wales Echo* went to Polly's, 69 High Street, Cowbridge, South Glamorgan. The young manageress bakes all the scones and cakes and serves an excellent selection of teas.

Castaways Antiques and Tea Shop, 32 Colleywell Bay Road, Seaton Sluice, Tyne and Wear, also won a Best Cuppa award, as did the National Trust's Periwinkle Cottage Tea Rooms, Selworthy Green, near Porlock, Somerset and The Folly Tree, Folly Lane, Petersfield, Hampshire.

Tea Council awards were also given to the charmingly old-fashioned Church House, Kington, Lyonshall, near Hereford, Worcestershire, and Court Barn Country Houses Hotel, Clawton, near Holsworthy, Devon, which was nominated by the compilers of *Let's Halt Awhile in Great Britain*, published by Ashley Courtenay. Another useful guidebook for travellers is Egon Ronay's *Just a Bite*, published by the Automobile Association.

Holiday-makers leaving from Heathrow Airport are lucky if they find themselves at Terminal 2 where The Runway provides several types of tea and won the Tea Council's Best Cup of Tea award for a British airport.

If you are in London and are feeling wealthy, go to the Ritz Hotel, Piccadilly, where you must reserve a table, and Le Meridien, Piccadilly Hotel. In both places you will be cocooned in a comfort that seems miles away from the bustle outside. Both of these hotels received Tea Council awards of Excellence.

WHERE TO BUY

Many of the ingredients mentioned in this book are available at good supermarkets. For more specialized herbs, and loose herbs rather than sachets, try your local health shop which can also supply water filters.

A remarkable variety of fine teas, available in small tasting samples, can be found at Whittards of Northgate Road, London, SW11 and the Conran Centre, Michelin House, Fulham Road, London SW3. (Coffee is also available from these suppliers.) Twining's Coffee House, 216 Strand, London WC2, offers a good selection of teas and coffee, as does Taylors Tea and Coffee Limited, Pagoda House, Prospect Road, Starbeck, Harrogate, Yorkshire and Taylors of Stonegate, York.

You can find marvellous teapots and jugs at the Tea House, Neal Street, Covent Garden, London; 7 Shreeves Walk, Stratford-upon-Avon and at 9 Golden Cross Walk, Oxford.

FOR FURTHER
READING

FOR THE LOVE OF FOOD
The Complete Natural Foods Cookbook: Jeanne Martin,
Ballantine Bks, N.Y.
HAMLYN'S GUIDE TO HERBS AND SPICES:
Monica Mawson, Hamlyn.
HEALING POWER OF HERBAL TEAS:
Ceres, Thorsons.
HERBS FOR HEALTH:
John and Rosemary Hemphill, Blandford Press.
HOME HERBAL:
Barbara Griggs, Pan Books.
NON DRINKER'S DRINK BOOK:
Betty Rollin, Frederick Muller.
Series of small books by Ceres, published by Thorsons, including:
HERBS AND FRUIT FOR SLIMMERS, HERBS FOR INDIGESTION.
TEA:
Eelco Hesse, Prism Press.
VOGUE GUIDE TO NON-ALCOHOLIC DRINKS:
Henry McNulty, Hamlyn.

ACKNOWLEDGEMENTS

Many thanks to the many people who helped with advice, particularly: Mark Evans, information officer for the National Institute of Medical Herbalists; Heath and Heather Herb Specialists; Giles Hilton, managing director of Whittard and Co. Ltd; Rona Hunnissett of the Fresh Fruit and Vegetable Information Bureau; the London Herb and Spice Co. Ltd; Sally Pattinson of the Japan Information Centre; the Tea Council.

RECIPE INDEX